my
DAD

For my dad, Leo—SQ
For my parents, thanks for everything—MR

Quarto is the authority on a wide range of topics.

Quarto educates, entertains and enriches the lives of our readers—enthusiasts and lovers of hands-on living.

www.quartoknows.com

First published in 2021 by words&pictures,
an imprint of The Quarto Group.
26391 Crown Valley Parkway, Suite 220,
Mission Viejo, CA 92691, USA
T: +1 949 380 7510
F: +1 949 380 7575
www.quartoknows.com

A CIP record for this book is available from the Library of Congress.

ISBN: 978-0-7112-5534-0

Manufactured in Guangzhou, China,
EB012021

9 8 7 6 5 4 3 2 1

MIX
Paper from
responsible sources
FSC
www.fsc.org
FSC® C124385

SUSAN QUINN

MARINA RUIZ

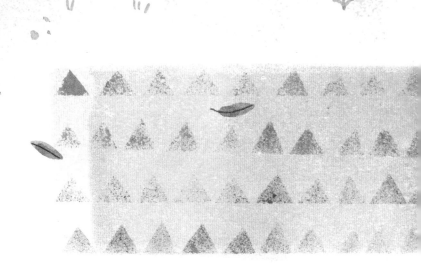

my

DAD

words & pictures

My Dad has never
been on a spaceship to
a galaxy deep in space.

Or been a secret agent,

or won a Grand Prix race.

He isn't a Super-Busy-Dad
always flying here and there—
but my Dad is...

Dad makes mornings special
because he loves to bake.

He makes *the best* cookies
and my favorite chocolate cake!

He gives me rides around the garden,
he grows vegetables all in a row.
And it's fun to pull up carrots,
shouting, "Ready! Set! GO!"

Dad says shopping is BORING,
but we never know who we'll meet...
when we pretend we're in the jungle,
looking for tasty food to eat!

Dad teaches me so many things;
like how to ride my bike,

what fun it is to roller skate...

and how to fly a kite.

He takes me
to soccer,
and watches
my team play.

Then cheers me up and makes me smile
when I've had a Really Bad Day.

Sometimes we go for picnics

and look for shells
beside the sea.

Then we watch the sunset
under the shade of a big tree.

If it rains, we splash through puddles,
stomp through leaves of gold and red.
And gaze at a colorful rainbow,
high above my head.

When it's cold we make a snowman,
and angels in the snow.

We pull the sled
to the top of the hill...

then

down

the

slope

we

GO!

Even when it's bath time,

Dad always makes me laugh.

We imagine lots of pirate ships

with billowing white masts.

Bedtime is for stories
and for snuggling up tight.
Then we count the twinkling
stars, before Dad says

"night
night!"

I love the time I spend with Dad—
he's the best a dad can be.
And every day is special
when it's just my Dad and me.